Elves and Fairies

by John Hamilton

Published by ABDO Publishing Company, 4940 Viking Drive, Suite 622, Edina, Minnesota 55435.
Copyright ©2005 by Abdo Consulting Group, Inc. International copyrights reserved in all countries.
No part of this book may be reproduced in any form without written permission from the publisher.
ABDO & Daughters™ is a trademark and logo of ABDO Publishing Company.

Printed in the United States.

Editor: Paul Joseph
Graphic Design: John Hamilton
Cover Design: TDI
Cover Illustration: *Gnomenclature* ©1995 Don Maitz
Interior Photos and Illustrations: p 1 *Tinkerbell the Fairy,* Corbis; p 5 *Fairy Rebels* ©2002 Don Maitz;
p 6 *Fairy Twilight,* Corbis; p 7 *Miss Pixie* ©1995 Don Maitz; p 8 *Mythology Abroad* ©1990 Don Maitz;
p 9 *Enter, an Elf in Search of a Fairy,* Corbis; p 10 *Mab Will Pinch Her by the Toe,* Corbis; p 11 *Applied
Mythology* ©1999 Don Maitz; p 12 *The Elf King Asleep,* Mary Evans Picture Library; p 13 *Borribles*
©1984 Don Maitz; p 14 Elves picking apples, Mary Evans Picture Library; p 15 top and bottom, Orlando
Bloom in *The Lord of the Rings,* New Line Cinema; p 17 *Mythology 101* ©1989 Don Maitz; p 18 *Pixie*
©1995 Don Maitz; p 19 *Elves Parachuting with the Aid of Thistledown,* Mary Evans Picture Library; p 21
Gnomenclature ©1995 Don Maitz; p 22 *Gn'obby Gnome* ©1995 Don Maitz; p 24 *Triumphal March of the
Elf-King,* Corbis; p 25 *Don't Look Down for a Bit,* Corbis; p 26 Frances Griffiths with fairies, Mary Evans
Picture Library; p 27 *Midsummer Eve,* Corbis; p 28 Elsie Wright with fairy, Mary Evans Picture Library;
p 29 *Fairy Wreath* ©1997 Don Maitz.

Library of Congress Cataloging-in-Publication Data

Hamilton, John, 1959–
    Elves & fairies / John Hamilton
       p. cm. — (Fantasy & folklore)
    Includes index.
    ISBN 1-59197-712-6
    1. Fairies—Juvenile literature. 2. Elves—Juvenile literature. I. Title: Elves and fairies. II. Title.

GR550.H267 2005
398.21—dc22

                           2004047747

CONTENTS

The Little People

airies are imaginary beings who appear in folklore all over the world. They are especially common in the folk literature of Western Europe and the Middle East. They are often called the little people, or the fair folk. Fairies come in many shapes and sizes. Both male and female fairies can be strikingly beautiful. Some are helpful and good, while others can be very bad.

Fairies are smaller than people, although some come close to human size. Quite often, though, fairies are very small, have pointed ears, and can flit about in the air on wings. Tinkerbell, from *Peter Pan*, is a kind of fairy called a pixie. She is an example of this kind of small fairy with wings.

Fairies live just beyond the detection of human beings. They often reside underground in magical earthen mounds, called fairy hills, or deep in enchanted forests, free from the gaze of humans. The little people like to dance at night around magical circles on the ground. These fairy rings can sometimes be detected during the day as circles of mushrooms, or where the grass is greener than the surrounding foliage. Sometimes humans stumble upon a fairy dance in progress and join in the fun. But time exists differently inside the magical fairy circle. Humans who think they've been dancing for an hour emerge from the circle to find that they've been gone for a whole year! So be careful if you're ever out in the woods and are tempted to join a fairy dance.

Far right: Fantasy illustrator Don Maitz's *Fairy Rebels.*

There are many kinds of supernatural creatures that are called fairies. They can be divided into two main groups. Trooping fairies live in communities and kingdoms much like humans. They make their homes in many different places. Elves and gnomes prefer deep forests, while pixies and other smaller fairies like flower gardens and meadows. Nymphs and sprites live close to water, while sylphs are spirits of the air.

The other group of little people are called solitary fairies. They prefer to live alone, and aren't associated with any particular place. Examples of solitary fairies include the Tooth Fairy, or the fairy godmother from the story of *Cinderella*.

Most fairies have some sort of magical ability. Fairies are shy and generally avoid humans. They can easily disguise themselves in order to stay hidden. However, most fairies are friendly if they do happen to meet people. Occasionally, they may even try to help people by doing simple chores, but this often ends poorly. In one fairy tale, a group of fairies takes pity on a poor tailor. Overnight, they secretly weave a coat made of gold thread, which they magically transformed from straw. But in the morning, as the sun rises, the gold thread turns back to straw!

Right: Fairy Twilight by John Anster Fitzgerald. *Far right: Miss Pixie* by Don Maitz.

6

Despite their general good nature, fairies are easily offended. They can make people's lives miserable if they feel insulted. It's never a good idea to talk badly of fairies, or worse, to say you don't believe in them.

Fairies can hurt people in many different ways. For example, they can send fog and storms down on unsuspecting travelers. Fairies have been known to lead weary travelers down a wrong path, or to pull chairs out from under people when they sit down. They are also said to steal babies in the night, leaving deformed changelings in their place. Even as recently as the turn of the twentieth century, some mothers in Great Britain tied down their infants in their cribs to prevent fairies from stealing away with their children in the night.

Despite these risks, many people go out of their way to find fairies. They are very difficult to spot because of their magic. Most fairies wear green clothes and can blend into the woods very easily. Humans can see them only rarely. Some people say that holding a four-leaf clover and lying very still will make fairies appear. There are many tales of people lying in enchanted woods suddenly being surrounded by dancing fairies.

Another way to spot fairies is to find a stone that has a hole in it. Stones from a stream or a river work well. If a person peers through the hole in the stone, it is much easier to see the fairies. The stone reduces their magical cloaking ability. It is almost like using a magical telescope just for finding fairies!

But, not everyone goes peeping through stones looking for fairies. Some people want nothing to do with fairies, or are afraid of the little people. Displaying crosses and ringing bells are well-known ways to ward off fairies. Hanging an iron horseshoe over the door of a home can keep fairies from entering. One legend says that if you pick a four-leaf clover, it will protect you from fairy spells.

Right: Mab Will Pinch Her by the Toe, by Cicely Mary Barker.
Far right: Applied Mythology by Don Maitz.

ELVES

Elves are a special kind of fairy. They are most common in the folklore of northern Europe, especially Germany, England, and Scandinavia. In German folklore, the word *elf* is often used to describe any kind of spirit creature.

Elves resemble tiny people. They have pointed ears, dress in green clothing, but have no wings. Elves possess very powerful magic. They can change into the form of animals, or disappear in a puff of smoke. Most elves are happy creatures who enjoy dancing and singing. They are nice to humans, but harmful if they are offended.

Elves are sometimes grouped into two categories. Light elves are good and kind, as well as bewitchingly beautiful. They can do favors for humans by doing chores in the middle of the night. Light elves have also been known to give good luck. People who help elves are sometimes rewarded with a pocketful of gold.

Left: The Elf King Asleep by Richard Doyle.
Far Right: Borribles by fantasy artist Don Maitz.

Dark elves are ugly and sinister. They often use their magic to evil ends. Farmers often complain of dark elves riding their horses all night until the poor animals are exhausted. Dark elves are also blamed for cows providing poor milk, for candles mysteriously blowing out, and for gusts of smoke billowing back down chimneys. Sometimes dark elves make farm animals ill by shooting tiny arrows called *elf-shot* at them.

In some places, especially rural Germany, elves were thought to cause disease in livestock and humans. They have also been known to sit on the chests of unwary sleepers and cause bad dreams. The German word for nightmare is *alpdrucken*, which means "elf-pressure."

In the Norse myths, light elves live in Alfheim, a land close to where the Norse gods dwell. Dark elves, on the other hand, live in Svartalfheim, a part of Midgard, the middle world of Norse culture. Humans, dwarfs, and giants also live in Midgard.

Left: Elves pick apples in this painting by Arthur Rackham.

Elves in The Lord of the Rings

Author J.R.R. Tolkien borrowed much from the Norse myths in his descriptions of elves in his epic trilogy, *The Lord of the Rings*. The elves in Tolkien's Middle Earth are human-sized light elves. The major elf characters include Legolas, Elrond, Arwen, and Galadriel. They are wise, immortal beings who can only die in battle. They live side-by-side with humans, but have a mistrust of dwarves. Elves love nature and live in or near enchanted woods. Their major cities include Lothlórien and Rivendell. *The Lord of the Rings* takes place during the Third Age, a time when elves grow tired of Middle Earth and sail to the Undying Lands for the rest of eternity.

Above and left: Orlando Bloom plays Legolas in director Peter Jackson's epic film trilogy *The Lord of the Rings*.

The Origin of Fairies

airies are found in the folk tales of many different cultures. The word fairy became commonly used during the Middle Ages. However, fairy-like creatures appeared in literature thousands of years before. The ancient Greek poet Homer wrote of sirens and nymphs in *The Iliad* and *The Odyssey*. Early Sanskrit poetry from India refers to celestial singers, while early civilizations on the Pacific Islands told of spirits resembling fairies. Even ancient Egypt had fairy-like creatures called Hathors.

Since so many cultures tell stories of fairies, it's natural to think that there might be a common origin to these creatures. But each culture has its own different account of the beginning of the fairy myth. It could be that fairy stories are so old that their beginnings have been lost to time. People have been telling fairy stories since before there was writing. As the tales were passed orally from one generation to the next, their origins slowly faded away. Today we are left with fairy folk tales and legends, which are almost impossible for scholars to trace and verify.

Far right: Mythology 101 by Don Maitz.

ELVES
COVER ART BY Maitz
ART DIRECTING BY DON PUCKEY
CONSULTING BILL FAWCETT

In Ireland, a country rich with fairy lore, the little people are thought to be all that remains of a conquered people called the Tuatha De Danaan, which means "People of the Goddess Dana." When ancient Celtic tribes first invaded Ireland, they drove the Tuatha into hiding. The pagan Tuatha gods also disappeared, taking their magic with them to live underground in ancient tombs and mounds hidden deep in the forests. As time passed, the Tuatha became smaller and smaller in the minds of the Celts, until they eventually were known as magical fairies.

The idea of a conquered race of people who fade away and shrink until they become magical creatures is a common thread in fairy mythology. It can be found in many cultures, from Europe, Africa, and Asia. It is one possible explanation of why fairy myths are so widespread. One variation on this theme is that local gods or spirits of nature have, over time, shrunk and diminished in power until they became the fairies that we know today.

Above: Elves Parachuting with the Aid of Thistledown by Ernest Aris. *Far left: Pixie* by Don Maitz.

Some cultures describe fairies as the souls of dead people who were not good enough to enter Heaven. They are doomed to wander over the Earth, only occasionally being seen by human beings. Other cultures believe that fairies were once angels, but were cast down from Heaven. They landed on Earth, and would do no harm as long as they were left alone.

Another explanation for the origin of fairies is that they have always been around and always will be. In Wales, the people believe that fairies are invisible spirits who live in a separate world all to themselves. Many other cultures have similar myths that are fascinating to explore and compare.

Fairies Around the World

Ireland

In the folk tales of Ireland, leprechauns are tiny little men who make shoes. There are several ways to spell the word leprechaun. The original is luchorpan, which means "little body." Leprechauns are usually described as little old men with long gray beards. They have long noses, and pointy hats and shoes. They usually wear green clothes. They can often be heard in the woods as they tap-tap-tap away at their shoe-mending chores. Leprechauns are known for jealously guarding their hoards of gold. They may reveal the location of their hidden gold if they are captured. But if their captors look away, even for an instant, the leprechauns will laugh and vanish into the air.

England and Scotland

Brownies are household spirits that live mainly in northern England and Scotland. They are very small and shaped like humans. Some are naked and shaggy, and others wear ragged brown clothes. Some brownies have no nose, and others have just two nostrils on their face. These helpful fairies perform many tedious chores for humans, such as sweeping, grinding grain, or churning butter. In return, human families give the brownies a bowl of cream or a freshly baked loaf of bread. It is considered good luck to have a brownie living in your house. However, brownies will undo all of their work and make a mess of things if they feel they've been criticized.

Far right:
Gnomenclature by
Don Maitz.

20

SOUTHERN ENGLAND

Pixies are a kind of trooping fairy that live in human-like communities. They can be found mainly in the folklore of southern England. Pixies are very small fairies with wings, red hair, turned-up noses and pointy ears. Pixies are similar to brownies because they help people with household chores and expect bowls of cream or freshly baked bread or cakes in return. Pixies can be mischievous. At night, they like to lead weary travelers down wrong paths until they become exhausted. This is where the phrase "pixie-led" comes from. Pixies sometimes live in communities underground, but many prefer flower gardens. People who accidentally stumble upon a pixie community often like to join in a pixie dance, but these people soon lose all sense of time, and may not leave until months or years have passed.

GERMANY

German folklore tells of kobolds, who act much like English brownies. Kobolds look like little garden gnomes. They have the faces of little old men and wear colorful clothing that includes a tall, pointed cap. Kobolds usually live in barns, or near the hearth area of a home. They are happy to do chores for deserving families. They don't expect much in return, except for a small portion of the family dinner. If they are not treated with respect, however, kobolds can turn mischievous toward their human hosts.

JAPAN

Kappa are evil fairies from Japanese mythology. They are small, monkey-shaped spirits whose name means "child of the river." They live in streams and ponds, and have scaly skin and webbed fingers. Kappa like to lure people into the water and eat them alive. Sometimes clever humans can negotiate with the Kappa and spare their lives. One trick is to bow in front of a Kappa. In Japanese society, even evil fairies must return bows. When a kappa bends over, water drains from his head. Since water is the source of the fairy's power, the kappa is helpless. This gives the human a chance to flee to safety.

Far left: Gn'obby Gnome by Don Maitz.

NIGERIA

In the Upper Niger region of Nigeria in Africa, an evil water spirit called Zin preys on unwary travelers. Simply looking at a zin can often be fatal. The name zin may come from the Arabic djinn, which is the name for fairy spirits that inhabit the Saharan regions of North Africa. In western culture, djinns are more commonly known as genies.

CANADA

Tales of fairies can be found in North America, too. Tootega is a female water spirit from the folk tales of the Inuit people of northern Canada. She appears as a little old woman who walks on the surface of the water. The Inuit people say Tootega lives in a little stone house on an island.

Far right: Don't Look Down for a Bit, by Florence Mary Anderson. *Below: Triumphal March of the Elf-King,* by Richard Doyle.

The Cottingley Fairies

Perhaps nowhere in the world have fairies been more popular than in England in the early 1900s. In 1917, two English schoolgirls played a practical joke that fooled many people. The two girls took photographs in the woods behind their home. The photos showed them playing and dancing with tiny winged fairies. People were astonished, and the controversy went on for more than 60 years until the girls finally admitted to the truth.

One of the girls was Elsie Wright. She lived with her parents in a small village called Cottingley. Sixteen-year-old Elsie was a former art student. She had also worked as a photographer's assistant. Elsie's 10-year-old cousin, Frances Griffiths, stayed with the Wright family during the summer of 1917, along with her mother.

The two girls often played near

Below: Frances Griffiths watches some of the fairies she and Elsie Wright used to play with in the woods near Cottingley, England.

a stream that ran through Cottingley Glen, the woods near the Wright's home. Frances' mother would often scold the young girl for coming home with wet and dirty clothes. She asked Frances why she spent so much time in the woods. Frances answered that she liked to play with the fairies who lived there.

One afternoon, Elsie borrowed her father's camera and went off to the woods with Frances. Later, as Elsie's father helped her develop the photographs in his darkroom, he was astonished to see a photo of Frances with several tiny fairies dancing around her.

Above: Midsummer Eve by Edward Robert Hughes.

More photos eventually surfaced of the wee folk dancing and frolicking with Frances and Elsie. At first, the families of the two girls thought it was all a joke.

By 1919, many people began taking the photos seriously. This was a time when "spirit photography" was very popular. Many unscrupulous crooks sold pictures of people with ghost-like dead relatives standing in the background. What people didn't realize was that the photos were double exposures, two pictures sandwiched together. Most people didn't know much about photography, and were easily tricked. The popular belief was that the camera could "see" things that human beings might miss.

Spiritualists, people who studied ghosts and other supernatural beings, took an interest in the Cottingley fairy photographs. Many photographic experts said the pictures were not faked. After examining the negatives, they declared that the images were not double exposures and that the negatives had not been tampered with in any way. Therefore, these people said, the photos had to be real.

In 1920, Sir Arthur Conan Doyle, the writer who created Sherlock Holmes, became interested in the Cottingley fairy photos. He used the images for an article he wrote in the Strand Magazine. The two girls were paid 20 pounds, about $38 in today's dollars, which was quite a bit of money in 1920. In the article, Doyle said he was "on his guard" about the photos. But as the years passed, it became clear that he was a true believer. He later wrote a book about the photographs.

In 1982, the girls finally confessed that it was all a prank that had gotten out of hand. They had wanted to tell the truth early on, but all the publicity had made it too difficult.

In a 1983 interview, Elsie explained how she and Frances made the photos. When Elsie's parents were out, she copied pictures of fairies from a book and mounted them on pieces of cardboard. The girls used hatpins to fix them in place and then took the photographs.

In 1997, the story of the Cottingley fairies hoax was made into a movie called *Fairy Tale: A True Story*. Stories of fairies continue to fascinate people all over the world. Many people believe these tales are absolutely true, while some say that fairies have never existed. However, fairies and elves will always be a very real part of folklore all over the world.

If You See A Fairy Ring.

If you see a fairy ring
In a field of grass,
Very lightly step around,
Tip-Toe as you pass,
Last night Fairies frolicked there
And they're sleeping somewhere near.
If you see a tiny fairy
Lying fast asleep
Shut your eyes
And run away,
Do not stay to peek!
Do not tell
Or you'll break a fairy spell
Author Unknown

Glossary

CELESTIAL

A being that lives in the sky or in heaven. Angels and some fairies are celestial beings. Celestial also sometimes refers to a physical object that is found in the universe, like a planet or star.

CELTIC

Refers to the people or the language of the Celts, who dominated the British Isles and parts of France and Scandinavia for hundreds of years before the Roman invasion and occupation of 43 A.D.

CHANGLING

A child that is secretly put in the place of another. Fairies were often said to replace normal human babies with deformed fairy infants.

FOLKLORE

The unwritten traditions, legends, and customs of a culture. Folklore is usually passed down by word of mouth from generation to generation.

GENRE

A type, or kind, of a work of art. In literature, a genre is distinguished by a common subject, theme or style. Some genres include fantasy, science fiction, and mystery.

INUIT

The native people of North America who inhabit northern lands from Greenland and eastern Canada to Alaska. They at one time were called Eskimos, but Inuit is now the preferred term.

MEDIEVAL

Something from the Middle Ages.

MIDDLE AGES
In European history, a period defined by historians as between 476 A.D. and 1450 A.D.

MISCHIEVOUS
Full of mischief, being annoying or harmful through playful tricks.

NEGATIVE [PHOTOGRAPHIC]
A piece of exposed and developed photographic film in which light areas and dark areas are reversed. For example, a bright light appears like a dark shadow on a negative. Negatives are used to make prints of a scene. Light shining through a negative exposes the image on a piece of photographic paper, which creates a positive print of the scene. Negatives can sometimes be altered to create things that were never in the original scene, like fairies or UFOs. Today most photo manipulations are created digitally using computer software like Photoshop.

NORSE
The people, language, or culture of Scandinavia, especially medieval Scandinavia.

ORAL
Communicating by using spoken language. Most folklore is passed down from generation to generation by oral tradition. This means the stories are spoken and remembered, not written down. The details may change slightly over the years, but the basic story elements remain the same.

PAGAN
Generally, a person who doesn't practice a widely recognized formal religion, such as Christianity, Judaism, or Islam. There are several definitions of the word pagan. In the context of this book, pagans are people who worship nature or the earth, such as druids or witches.

SANSKRIT
The classical Old Indic language of India, developed from about the 4th century B.C. onward. Sanskrit has been used in many important literary works.

SPIRIT PHOTOGRAPHY
A trick used by criminals and hoaxers of the early 1900's, in which photographic negatives were altered so that a picture seemed to show ghostlike images. Photography was a new art form, and many believed it was possible for photos to show things the human eye couldn't normally see. Many people paid large sums of money to have spirit photographs taken in order to contact long-dead relatives.

INDEX

A
Africa 19, 24
Alfheim 14
alpdrucken 14
Arwen 15
Asia 19

C
Canada 24
Cinderella 6
Cottingley, England 26,
    28
Cottingley Glen 26

D
Doyle, Sir Arthur Conan
    28

E
Egypt 16
elf-shot 12
Elrond 15
England 12, 20, 23, 26
Europe 12, 19

F
Fairy Tale: A True Story 28
28

G
Galadriel 15
Germany 12, 14, 23
Great Britain 9
Griffiths, Frances 26, 27,
    28

H
Holmes, Sherlock 28
Homer 16

I
Iliad, The 16
India 16
Inuit 24
Ireland 19, 20

J
Japan 23

L
Legolas 15
Lord of the Rings, The 15
Lothlórien 15

M
Middle Ages 16
Middle Earth 15
Middle East 4
Midgard 14

N
Nigeria 24
North Africa 24
North America 24

O
Odyssey, The 16

P
Pacific Islands 16
Peter Pan 4

R
Rivendell 15

S
Scandinavia 12
Scotland 20
Strand Magazine 28
Svartalfheim 14

T
Third Age 15
Tinkerbell 4
Tolkien, J.R.R. 15
Tooth Fairy 6
Tuatha De Danaan 19

U
Undying Lands 15
Upper Niger 24

W
Wales 19
Western Europe 4
Wright, Elsie 26, 27, 28